Children's Book

Children's Book

Gene Geter

Writers Club Press
San Jose New York Lincoln Shanghai

Children's Book

Writers Club Press
an imprint of iUniverse, Inc.

For information address:
iUniverse, Inc.
5220 S. 16th St., Suite 200
Lincoln, NE 68512
www.iuniverse.com

Any resemblance to actual people and events is purely coincidental.
This is a work of fiction.

ISBN: 0-595-22705-8

Printed in the United States of America

Contents

Children's Book

If you want to be truly free,
You will read on
Life is just like a book
It has a beginning and an end
But as of today,
We're still in the heart of the book

Let's think about this
What kind of book are you?
Are you a dictionary?
Are you a novel?
Are you a photo book?
Are you a religious guide?
Are you a pornography volume?
The best book to be is a children's book

Why?
A children's book never deals with time
A children's book is about happiness
A children's book is about living life without stress
A children's book is enjoying real freedom
The freedom that the supreme universe gave to all of us

Look at the children around the world
They always have smiles
They always have fun

The world is extra great to them
They always know how to play

Life is a book
The best book to be is a children's book
Children live in the present
Children know nothing of the past
They know nothing about the future
They only know about this minute and they execute it well

We can learn a lot from children
Because children understand the word love
They never take it for granted like adult humans
Children can tell someone that they love someone
Without any thought or shilly-shallying
Children melt into the one they love

If the growing up book takes us away
From the freedom of being ourselves,
If running wild is gone because we are older
And have tons of responsibilities,
Then, the best book to be is a children's book

Wouldn't you think?

Don't you want to be free again?

To be true again?

Like an animal again?

Like a flower again?

The Mayor

———— ∞ ————

Doing it for that soul
Running again
Doing it for those legs and feet
This time the win will be
Campaigning to be the true love of that mind
That fine body with the sun-drenched on that line
Up and down the future mayor will speak
This voice will be bleak

Doing it for that kiss
Waiting again
Waiting some more
Doing it for that hair
Soon to brush and style
Running to be the end love of that future
That past which never been in the suture
See the mayor work the floor
This impact will be more and more

Doing it for that soul
Running again
Doing it for those legs and feet
This time the win will be
Campaigning to be the true love of that mind
That fine body with the sun-drenched on that line

Children's Book

Up and down the future mayor will speak
This voice will be bleak

Doing it for that title
Craving it for thus years
Doing it for that worth
The reward it represents
The destiny it embroiders
Determined to be the definitive love of this generation
To be the key to this final revelation
Willing to be higher than temptation or simple lust
Fighting to be the piece of the pie, some of the crust

Doing it for that soul
Running again
Doing it for those legs and feet
This time the win will be
Campaigning to be the true love of that mind
That fine body with the sun-drenched on that line
Up and down the future mayor will speak
This voice will be bleak

Doing it for the theme
Hear it for the mayor
The confetti is falling everywhere
The sponsor is very ecstatic with all the hype
Walking proud to get closer to that mind
See the mayor in the shy distance
About to step on the path to that closed sensation
Doing it for that flower to blossom
Get that infancy running again like an opossum

All hail the mayor for that mind
Accept the rank for that heart
Doing it so it will be done well
To feel the essential best of heaven
Beyond the sevens and elevens
The angels and golden harps
Doing it to rid all carp
The mayor's running again

The Great Ones

I'm only an alien to you
I was put on this earth to rule what I gotta rule
Touch you lover with an impromptu kiss
Rub all your dreams true as I adventure you
Through and through
I was planned to do the plan too

Do you see that you need me?
Finally admit it that you circulate me when you're thinking
Like the essence of blood
Realize that you breathe me when you avoid me
Understand to get me while I still want you
Before I wake up and not want you
Do something to only show me
That you know I'm the way to your eventual destiny

You are this, this close to me and you don't even know
You might have this intemperance for punishment
You are a fool to miss me so many times
This is your last chance or my last stanza
To embrace destiny's handsome reward that's me
All the evil banter we inflicted on ourselves
When all we truly wanted was love
If I love you,
You will love me
Simply said

But not simply executed
I realized the words of Don Miguel Ruiz
That you only do as I do anyway
So I will appreciate you for now on
And you cannot not appreciate me
As long as I'm doing whatever act to you first
You will follow me

Folklore is folklore
But our tale is one legend not documented
Maybe the end of our final chapters are impending
I really don't want to become a literary tragedy
By a famous present author just embellishing
On a past author's masterpiece using different names
Like Anthony and Cleopatra
We were never them and we will never be them
We have to be us once we find us
I just can't wait to start loving you

I see the dream
It comes to me in the millions around the world
That dream is a birth of a preordained dawn
The birth is about a love given to us
From the curtain behind the cosmos
The love we hold and not use
Is one of the great ones
It's the love that you see in movies
The love you see in plays
It's the love others grow jealous of when seen
This love will kill us if we don't try it
This love is breaking its last spine for us
Still, we won't try it

We won't even talk about it
I don't know what in the hell is wrong with us

Fate is aware of us
We are not aware of fate
I know that I want you as my woman now
But you wouldn't know a good man
If God told you personally
The problem remains that you won't declare the truth
I was unbreakable until I met you
I'm stronger because of you
I can't break this fate
You can't break this fate
Trust me, the universe will compensate us wonderfully
If we pair off
We are absolutely victorious together
We are nothing without the other my love

The Energy Behind Negativity

———— ∽ ————

Being positive is not asking
To convert to a religion
Nor is it a belief
Nor should it be taken as
We are believers of any faith
Did we ever think why we are so negative?
Why do we think things we always fail?
We don't want to be positive
Because we know it will be negative?
What kind of common sense is that?
The answer is it is not common sense at all
It's just an excuse to lose

For some, we don't want to be positive
Because we don't believe in unworldly forces
Believe it or not
As much time and energy we use
To say everything is coincidental or accidental
And not by destiny or fate
Is giving as much time and energy to saying it does not
Not to reference The Bible as a funny story,
But being negative is like trading Jesus for Lucifer
Do we really want to do that?
No matter what we think, religion or not
There's something out there

So why not be positive?
To not be positive and stay negative
Is the reason why we should be positive
Why dwell the opposing force?
Being negative owns more problems
Than we can handle
We were born from positive births
And if we don't like feeling negative,
We don't have to be
And yet, if we are still negative
We don't have to be still
We don't have to be anything we don't want to be
So be positive, agreed?

Hear Quiet Say Hush

———— ∞ ————

Can I wash your feet?
Or simply kiss them upon a fancy float?
Your eyes reveal a gloat
A head nod of okay to satisfy you
As I satisfy myself
By pleasing you

Can I tell you about my travels?
And how each day unravels
The pure essence of my secret fate?
Like heaven's gate,
I step closer to opening them sound
I spread plus signs to all who is around
Or who's not
Still I spread the plus signs across the world

Can I hold your hand?
As I point to beauty in every direction we go?
Funny, I point to wonderful nature
As wonderful nature points to you
Beauty understanding beauty
You understanding me
I understanding you
Perfect harmony is beautiful, too

Can I wash your locks?
As I unlock the truth of your deepest spirit?
I can't see it
I hear it
It's very low
It wants to explode
Am I right?
Like light, it wants to burst out bright
Well, it is light
Surely, I wouldn't mind to honor the light
Lay beside it all night

Could we stay together just like this?
Enjoying this dreamlike rapture?
Enjoying this soporific midst?
I decided you are the mist
I want to be secluded by
There's no way to deny
You and I

After I dry your locks,
I want to show you the grotto
By the way of piggyback ride
I made dinner for you
And candles by hand
To use in honor of your arrival
We are so right
Like the wind has been all day

Nicole, tell me your favorite song
I will sing to you on our way
Close your eyes

The trip will be smooth
Soothe into my words
Become one with your surroundings
Do you feel the energy?
Of everything and everyone?
Do you feel the rays in the clouds?
Do you feel it all?
You do?
Don't you want it all?
You do?
I want you
Do you want me?
You do?
I want you again

Here we are
I hope you like it
I thought of you when I discovered it
It's very peaceful as you can hear
It's so quiet here,
You could almost hear quiet say hush
Excuse me if I stare at you too long
Or too weird
You are just such a daydream
With you,
I stopped being surprised by the precious gifts
That's sent to me
With you, I know why I receive gifts
With you within my time
I know tomorrow will be more special than today
I found you by the grace of God
Though you weren't lost

You were part of the plan
Never was I once worried
I knew you before I met you
Are you happy, baby?
You were always happy?
I'm happy, too
Did you say you love me?
Don't cover up your smile
I love your smile
And I love you, too

Forgive Me Superstar

———— ∞ ————

I plan to say your name a lot
Until your first anniversary arrives
In the form of superstar
Why am I acting like you are God or something?
It might sound like this is in vain
But I have words to say,

I have a connection to you
Forgive me superstar
I might be crazy
Or I might be right
I know my psyche
I know myself
I have a connection to you

Why did you die?
I feel like I should have known you more
I hope you weren't my soulmate
I'm afraid you were a piece of my puzzle
That I won't figure out
Are you talking to me in my dreams?
My spiritual self hangs out with you
Across the great divide

Could you just be celebrity images in my head?
Could it be the bad food I devour before I crash?

Children's Book

I'm giving up plum wine and chunks of cheese
It's making my nocturnal reality gone vinegary
Forgive me superstar
I know you have better things to do
In your true destiny in the heavenly beyond

Pen & Poison Ink Letter

Before I am finished
This could turn out to be a term paper
Always thinking and writing about you
And you and you and you and you
Oh, today, I am through
I'm sorry, but I have to kill you

In pen with poison ink
I want you so dead now
I don't care no more
Every letter and word will feel your blood
Trust me this affecting you a lot new
You won't have me to rely on any longer
If I could slap you with ink,
How would it sound?

Once I get my pen with some poison ink
A stiff you will be in my fatal tour de force
Farewell worthless skin and bones
Read these letters and acquire a heart attack on me
Please?
Read these words and stop breathing
Won't you?
Gratify me in death where you could not in life
That would mean so much to me, he, hee

Children's Book

Poison ink will cut you into strips
Before I am finished
This could turn out to be a term paper
Always thinking and writing about you, you, you
Oh, I am through
I'm not sorry, I want you gone
From the rest of time
From the rest of mind
Out of my soul
Out of my heart

I know I'll get you out in pen with poison ink
I know I should be drinking Egyptian chamomile
I blame you for stress, agony and affliction
The mental masturbation
You turned me into a bad man
Why did you change me?
Sometimes I want to slam your small head against a fucking wall
With long, sharp spikes to see it puncture your skull, ha, ha
I see you got me acting up again
I will keep a grip of composure, ha, ha

If I had some balls,
I'd kill you for real, muddy bastard fuck
With a machete and bury you myself
I would not need any help
It would be my pleasure
I would not mind, not even a not very
So I will continue until I complete this poison ink type letter
I am planning to stick a gun hard into her cold heart

And make her read it out loud, naked and wet
Connected to electric devices strapped to her hands and legs
Just to be content, ha, hee

Hell

Heaven is when you leave this place
This place called Earth
Called Earth because it is hell for sure
For sure it is just look around
Look around and you will see hell
See hell now

The good die young
Die young is a present or a blessing
A blessing because this is truly hell
Truly hell I live among the evil
The evil all around must mean that I'm bad too
Bad too I'm still here
Still here I don't want to be anymore
Be anymore

The Dolls And Their Houses

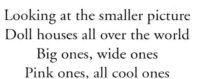

Looking at the smaller picture
Doll houses all over the world
Big ones, wide ones
Pink ones, all cool ones
Some parents have a problem
With their kids playing with white dolls

Some parents don't care if their kids
Play with white dolls
As long as they have black dolls, too
So why is it that some people get upset?
When they see white kids play with black dolls?
Why does race have to be a part of anything?
I don't understand and yet, I do
Let's just see what the dolls have to say about this

Don't say anything, nothing
When the dolls and their houses
Come alive all over the world
Wanting to fight you parents
Disfigure your face in dark alleys
Or in the very bright, broad daylight
Making you run from plastic stuff and silicon

Better

How you living life?
Is it better than the dreams?
Are you still feeling rotten?

I guess your slice of the pie is not tasting cream

Do you think there's a remedy?
Or something you can take?
Like trying Fenugreek
Or even Daily Detox?

Feeling better is sometimes a paranoid stake

Does it hurt trying things without belief?
Or does it hurt even more that you're doing it to feel better?
Do you hate the mental chaos?
The one that all human beings ensue?
Do you get bothered that love is still not around?

And love's still not here again for you?

Life really sucks so much
Why do we live it?
Don't be afraid of death, they say
But death never gave me a reason to die
Aren't you still waiting for birth to tell you why you were born?

Would it make you feel better knowing a little bit more?

And if you say yes,
Then you have to think about something...
Would you really feel better?
Not really
Because knowing why is knowing all of why
And not just a piece

The Lost Orphans Of Queens County

Most of them are dead
The ones that are not
Are nearly

This county has turned its back
On the innocent
Because they can't be raised by the guilty

The soldiers are here
They make the lost orphans uneasy
It is truly a pity

They want to wet their pants
The soldiers make them think about something
They can't think about in the county

Keep the lost orphans free of the mystery
Not any children's books will ever speak of this
Throughout history

The Date

It didn't take long for the crown princess
To want me outside her jurisdiction
Our eyes tell the story of crave
We look in our eyes all the time
The power is there
We dip around the land
From pub to club to bistro
Someone famous is in town
And we heard her play the piano
The fun began at that moment
Telling me stories of happy and unlucky
I'm feeling happy or sorry for her
But wanting her in that place
She kisses my smiling line
And my feelings are divine
And I blush and blush
Because she hits a crush
She places her leg over mine
Then, I want her so profound

She invites me back to her lair
She says tomorrow she will be queen
Of all she surveys but tonight,
She will be the meretrix of my fantasies
We both know when tomorrow arrives,
This will never happen again

The date we will remember forever
She turns on the music box
She puts on her ever fancy jewelry
You know, from her strong box
I said I want you made up
When I turn you out
She says close my eyes
I have to comply
She will be the queen tomorrow

She says she gets the nastiest
Whenever she's around me
Sometimes, she wants to do everything and anything
But what should we do first?
If only it could be rehearsed
I get the lights
I light the candles
She turns down the bed
This is between ourselves
In the detection of red
I want her animal support
I ask for the professional
Heard she does it very well
So she starts and it's a knockout
How the fingers, the mouth and the lips
Work so sexy with the saliva

Raise A Flag

———— ∞ ————

Your flag
My flag
It doesn't matter what flag
Just raise a flag

Every country love your country
Your flag
My flag
It doesn't matter what flag
Just raise a flag
And flag your flag

Your flag is you
My flag is me
Our flags is our image
Show that your image still has hope
By seeing the flag

Until The Stars And Moons Burn Out

Fresh brainy aleck
Stamped by fate since birth
The forever and the magic card
Hidden in this sweet love deck
Someone has to shuffle
Thus
Until it's done right
Until the stars and moons burn out
Most of the universe will be pooped
By the time the truth is discovered
In another terminology,
When will Eve finally stop fearing Adam's love?
Like she fears God's wrath?

Magic Letters

The bionic ocean blue
In the forever coldness
Divided in the middle by counterfeit time
No chase to enjoy some plum wine
Still a dream summons the very sweetest taste

A knockout beatific creature
That can part the line of inner hips across the pendulum waist
Graced behind the sunshine
The intimate face of a diamond with eyelashes
Parked new confidence in the subterranean search for loyalty

Hope needs desire and crave wants feeling
While wish urges result and ask prompts question
For the experience to extend at least once more
The measure wants to rate performance
And the greatest delight must be accomplished

Again and again and again
Because in this pleasantry game
The Xs are required about three
Not necessarily the Os
But the Zs happen automatically
After all the Os are gone

To Peruse You

———— ∞ ————

Love sees the blues too
Love feels the booze and distorted hues
Love doesn't know when to snooze
Love refuses to lose
To peruse you

Love takes the abuse
Love fights the ruse
Love wears big shoes
Love never takes a cruise
To peruse you

Love wants to choose
Love focuses and infuse
Love reviews to never reuse or misuse
Love likes to stay new
To peruse you

Heck
Love is deep

The Vanilla Via The Gold

You don't let some women go
That's like handing out gold ingots
You just don't
Sometimes women don't think
Does she really think,
I came down here for the weather?
It may be nice in the villa
The cool light rain scintilla is a thriller
I see some judicious gorillas
But I'm here for the vanilla via the gold
I have been told not to be so bold
I didn't hold up to the bargain
Pardon all the quarrels that were old
They weren't sold fast enough
I don't regret what I had done
I will get back my fun
Walking up and down the sun without me
As if she had never knew me
Sue me, I'm a man
Acting briefly as a boy with a sex toy
Her way of life gets me forward
Because she is straightforward
Before I wasn't ready
I'm ready today
I hope she hears me tonight
I don't believe in too late

After my session with Dr. Phil O. Sophical
I'm having astrophysical insights
At midnight
When she's not in her room
I feel the peak of doom
Wondering if she's alone in drink
Or with someone horny else
I love that girl
And she's not here to hear it
Or witness the tears to feel it
Fall from my auburn face
This looks like my brightness now
Nine hours later in happy approach
All I got is dried rain plus sticky hide
I want to be mad like an alligator
I'm not a player hater
She's not mine at this time
I can't act like she is
She was once the treasure of me
She's always the state of pretty
I'm pretty stupid to let her go
I won't let her go again
I'm going to beg for a long time
That she will take me way back
Hi, baby
We need to natter
Why are you looking at me like that?
I have seen this look prior to this day
The vanilla via the gold

And A Wake For Time

I'm dying
I just found out
I mean, not right now
Although one day I will
I thought death paid me a visit this morning
And you were at the funeral alone
I guess it was all a dream for me
Yet, a superstar died very young
A friend of mine died too
Others dying as well or dead in the trouble
Or not being there for my niece
I have to appreciate each day forever
The sun is up
As I write this
The moon is down
My love is still all around
My soul is strong though
No matter what
Even if it's not served to any woman right now
Love that is
It's cool
I'm lying
It's not cool at all
Then again, I know you

You are a wall
That won't fall
You're feeling me
As much as I'm feeling you
I'm just not feeling this
When are we just going to give it up?
You've shared relations with me
Whether a wise choice or not
Whether right or wrong
Relations still took place
Hard to be friends with you
When I see so much more in you
I can't go back
I can't erase
I'm dead if I say something or nothing
I want more
I mean I want everything
Or nothing at all
I don't have time for this nonsense
And girl,
You give me a call
When you know what you want to do
When you want everything too
I just want to love you to the fullest
Until then,
Wake the fuck up silly smart!
And a wake for time

The Ignored

—————— ∞ ——————

What happened reverence?
What has happened in humankind today?
But chaos has a sweet new visage
When they destroyed the human shop
Do you know what I'm talking about?

I just can't beam today
I just can't sob tomorrow
I just can't subsist in yesterday
I can't go around accurate now
How could so many die?
Why?

I felt the lost lives of all the people
The unthinkable death
I'm so unbalanced
I don't know how to be
I don't know what to be
I'm immovable
Just so bare and brainless

Revenge is deeply masked during me
Although I know it's not precise
I just want to live and gain
But how do you beat the ignored?
If we thought about the hidden in the universe,

We wouldn't be having this quandary
Reverence is so far-flung in the out there
I'm confident we can find away to harness it
To be sincere

Cereal

Jenny Judy asked her mommy
For her favorite cereal
Her mommy said,
"No, you eat too much cereal."

Jenny said, "No, no, I don't."
Her mommy said,
"You do, you do.
Now go outside and play."

Jenny went outside
Still hungry
She thought, it wasn't funny
Later that morning, she saw her friends,
Richard Red and Samantha Blue
They smelled like frosted fruit

"We just finished eating
our fourth bowl of cereal,"
they said.
"And guess what?
Your mommy gave it to us!"

"It's not fair, it's not right,"
Jenny cried, running back inside.
"Why mommy? Why?"

Her mommy said,
"Because they helped me clip my toes."

Sodom & Gomorrah

———— ∞ ————

Finally, it's time to get this shit out in the open
I want you so there
And I want you open and wet and moaning
I want you floating on my dandelion stokes
Until you choke on the good hit
What?

Like rape, I want to snatch your clothes off
Invent handcuffs out your bra
Pull you to me and throw you hard on a flowery bed
And sex you relentlessly
Until you bleed the color of the sea Moses parted
Do you hear me?

Massage you with my spit and watch it drip
Off your skin, your lips and trimmed pubic area
Until the lust jams us in sexual hysteria
Feeling the power of a diseased malaria
You are mine, sweet Gomorrah
And I'm fucking you
And I'm freaking you for the you I want to get in

Honey, don't you even move
I'm sure to soothe you in every point
My dick is the joint
And soon, you will be taking a hit

Because this erected shit is equipped
To rip through your shy channels
This fuck is not about to handle
The coming sure to commence
In care of your horny expense
Baby, baby, please
You just can't stifle this mental rifle

If we could just go back to that night
When Sodom & Gomorrah weren't quite right
So you can understand this good heat
When I beat inside of you
Like I am fighting you
I'm just trying to win
So you can get off on the zesty orgasm
Still feeling the intimate sarcasm
But you are in this prime position for phantasm
Feel this coarse melody, soon to roast
I don't want to boast
I am in the coast, in the country
In your greenery of sweet meadows
As your insides feel the chunky honey
I'm not funny
I'm just canny or cunning
Yet, hunting the pussy
Like I can't get enough
Like marshmallows
Or too many games of Othello
Seeing as when we fuck, it's like fucking crazy
I feel like I'm working hard and still lazy
I'm in a daze from your maze
That amazes me when I blaze

I tweak your nipples to ripple
I slap your behind, why?
It's just fucking fine
It's just so smooth like a groove
That you hear on the radio from a cool night
I feel your shiver
I feel your fright
I'm laughing, your pussy's bright
Exactly the color I waited for all night
Now you are so ripe
I did damn good with the pipe
So girl, just flow with me in the air
Like a kite
Get high and don't deny
This fuck like induced with drugs
We bug from the jug
Make sure you fucking hold back on the lug

Rat

Get away from my cat, rat
Stop chasing my cat
My cat is not a rat
My cat should be chasing you rat
Get away from my cat, rat
Get back rat
Go chase another cat, rat
Or chase another rat, rat

Undertow

———— ∞ ————

Never really meant to be that nasty in the past
But you make me feel so devilishly heavenly
Since you took that quite bite
I've been waiting to take a bite too
The one from you

What it really comes down to
I want to make very slow love to you
You don't understand the chemistry I possess
It is like the undertow
Just when you don't expect it
Here it comes my love it sweeps you
So watch out for this love that swipes you
Into a cherubic place you've never been
Girlfriend sing sweetly amen

Emendations

Like a wink,
Emendations will father
The willingness is the instantaneous completion
Something wrong
Automatically becomes right with emendations
When the soul says yes,
The mind will follow
Making emendations every second,
Every minute, every hour
Whenever it has

The Meeting

—————— ∞ ——————

The days into the nights
The crust into the lust for the must
To crush into the rush into flush
For the dust to in bust
I won't rust

The suns and the moons
The blooms into the looms into grooms
Or brides into rides that slides
For the glide that guides into hides
You will provide

The occurred incurred this evening
The intricate meeting
Vaginal secretion understanding semen
To be heating in this room alone
When we are defeating what we are beating

Give in or just give up
The waiting cups without hiccups
Full of yups into your pups
I can erupt
You can erupt
The end of these weird days
Divided up

Along into the strong to belong
Snapping mental the thong
To the song
I will dong you or prong
All night long and along
Like I said into the strong to belong
Are you gong?

So just whack to this crack
Put your back to my axe
Make love for it's black
Watch me shellac what's intact
I am your hack
Won't you take a tap of this tack?
Sit your stuff on my stack
And let's get on this rack
To this gender jack
So we can smack and snack
Each other juicy Eve
You have me on your sleeve
Get your morning mack
Sure you will quack like a quack
To my physical aphrodisiac
I want to hear your naughty yak
Are you ready for the attack?
Hit me back

A Reign Of Certainty

———— ∞ ————

Yesterday,
She gave me a little river to see
A passionate opening to a new day
A special feeling she sprang from me
Let's see what happens next

The night was full of dreams
An esplanade engaged us and waged us
The bodies were cold and heat ravaged as well
The way of the thoughts consumed just by sitting close
If only she would propose
If only she would converge the natural desire

Living in that yesterday all the time now
How I lapse it from mind
I don't
I will not
I adore it too much
Because I want to be adored
I think

The Worth

At vaginal birth
The institute gave the worth
Complete love
Without dearth
The worth is true mirth
The worth is part of the girth
It's everywhere on Earth
Still in Perth
Your berth in the worth
Is to reclaim a mental rebirth
Deliver the worth
Unearth the greatest love without dearth

To Play

———— ∞ ————

She waited for my eyes to go back in my head
Knowing her eyes were doing so mentally
But the truth is I let down a wall
To get a wall let down from her

Then two walls went down
We were physical without being physical
We were sexual with the windows to our souls
She saw a sneak peek of philosophical fine-tune
And I saw her on the inside
Wanting to await an empty room

Her directions was to play
And I played
I gave her my hidden faces
As she described mystical wishes
That made me want to gracious the real play

Such when the little self-worth erupted
Her hidden love for the play ravaged her significantly
She didn't want to show her admittance
Even now her deviance proved to be bigger than any denial
To date, if she ever wants to play all over again
I wouldn't mind seeing her eyes outdistance

The Military Of Light

Lead them over every bridge
In every land
Within every world
For the last battle
Don't worry
Darkness is troubled
Their hiding places are narrow
Like a shadow
The military of light will expose them all

Do you see them?
They walk tall
In the colors of angels
Without arms
They carry simply their gifted minds
Somehow, darkness thought they were in control
Once more, they were blinded by the light
The military of light that is
This war should have never left heaven
But it will end here on Earth
What are we fighting for?
We are fighting for love
Unconditional love
We fight in the name of God
In defense of his laws
Bringing the truth back

For the young boys and girls
To keep the new generations pure
Bare with us
The dream of an impeccable Earth will be
Sooner than the future knows

Re-missed

———— ∞ ————

Using the word remissed in this one
Actually re-missed
Because remissed means what I'm not saying
So re-missed
Let me enlighten

Ever miss the sun when it doesn't shine for like 14 days?
Ever miss a drink when you can't buy a glass?
Ever miss a kiss from someone you never had?
That's re-missed
It's missed when it's not really yours to grab
It's like you went to the far, far back of the garden
For the last few weeks
You are re-missed
Every splinter of the era
Missed and re-missed equally sliced

Missing the foster that once was the light
Re-missing the dream of it every time
Hoping or knowing it will return
Feeling its walk back to the road it left
Coming back nearer than I could invent
The love of all of you all the time
It's re-missed

Just deeply re-missed
Could you blow me a bright, ashen kiss?
I'm sure it won't take long to reach my countenance

Blowing Tops

————— ∞ —————

Mountain high
These eyes are the sky and seagulls fly
White clouds
White water noise
Sounds of the grand sand land
Skin of the woman's woman
Lips of the power admirer
An experiment only
For the two commonly lonely

Mind to the hilltop intermittent light
On mountain high
Loads the soul and heart with sweet rage
To bare the power rare
Soon to blast serious passion fast
The intimate stratagem of blowing tops
It is a possible in reality new days
Behold those lips of the power admirer
Gifted with long lasting, hard-earned, radiant desire fire

Mary Magdalene

In this poem,
The boy gets the girl
Hopefully,
In real life,
After you read this,
I hope to have you finally

Your sisters said it a long time ago
That we were meant to be together
I just laughed and I still laugh
But I also think about it
I hate to admit that you make me melt

You have to admit
That I get under your skin in a good way
You just haven't realized it yet
You will one day
I'm telling you this now
So I can embark the spell verbally into the universe

I have this feeling sometimes
You are too proud to reveal how you feel
You rather run from the truth
Than face it

After you were a prostitute
You're probably thinking I don't respect you
Or I won't respect you

Sometimes we take on the characteristics of people in The Bible
Remember when Jesus met Mary Magdalene?
She was a prostitute
But he never saw her as a prostitute
Some people believed that Jesus loved this woman
And if you were my woman
I would love you
Because I love you
I would never see you as you once were ever

Binoculars To An Old Man's Desire

Hope he doesn't get his eyes stuck in them
Pushes his soul into a larger vision
Struggles to see all of it
To see all of her
Blood pressure too high
Pills will not help him any
He needs to breathe
If he could breathe,
He would enjoy the view
He struggles on
To see much of nothing
What he looks for is all in his mind

White Boyfriend

───── ∞ ─────

I laugh behind the laugh
Thinking of she
She went out there
Tons of white men right here
A white boyfriend is not very special

He looks at she different like a trophy
Because of black legs and ass
Love that's not enough
I look at she different too
Like ice cream

Except I can truly enjoy the flavors
This is a warning white men
Leave our Nubian queens alone
You have nothing going on with them
You will never be in the same light
Enough among dipping and diluting the true superior race
This jungle fever bull manure must cease

Corrupted, I Think

———— ∞ ————

Maybe I'm just a bad writer
All my life
I thought I could make the difference
In a person's eyes
Maybe I'm writing enigmatic valentines to God

I told this girl once
I miss seeing you more
You know we're fun
I promise you the best fun
And when I need someone to talk to
I have you
Just please be my buddy
Spend a little more time with me
I know times are changing
But when you are busy running
I have no one to talk to
I miss when you used to call me up often
I still want to share my thoughts with you
And talk about doing something anything
This goes to the one with the initials DCL
You are my friend

I have learned
I haven't changed one individual's thought
I wish I could dream about roving

Then dream about this and that
I wish I could stop feeling this error
I want to have better thoughts now
I deserve better and more
I'm corrupted, I think
I can't get back
Maybe I should just die
Nothing has ever worked out

Peep Show

———— ∞ ————

Just wanted a weird experience today
Maybe something to write about
Or something to drain this overpowering lust
So I walked until I found a peep show
With live girls in the morning time

One caught my eye
Or I caught her earnings
Blond light skinned black girl wanted my business
She told me about the peep show and the glass booth
So I went for the $20 masturbation
The other choices sounded lame

I pay her $20
I enter the boy room
She enters the girl room
I pay an added $5
For 5 minutes in the booth
I can see her
She says come on, pull down those pants

I obeyed
She takes off her bra and panties
She squeezes her juicy melons on the chair
She spreads her legs and makes that pussy jump
She's rubbing it now and it seems so phony

Children's Book

While I jerk off to all of this and more
I know it's just her job
She probably thinks I'm an idiot
I think she's an idiot, too
But we both get what we sought after
I delude you not
True story

Read This Woman

After I say every word
I will fall in love with the poet
I will realize now when I didn't know it
That the poet who wrote it
Becomes the one who beholds it
The love I've always wanted
That I silently cry for in the meadows of deliberation
From morning, noon and night
Bring my sex to this poet's light
Let my thoughts be of him all the time
Until I tell him what's on my mind
This man, the poet is the man I've always needed
I will see him for everything he wants from me
I will tell him after I say every word
That I want him, the poet
I will tell him to love me like I have never been loved
I will feel his love all around me
I will feel his love more if I don't embrace this love spell
I will feel his soul on my body when I sleep at night
I will feel him forever until I give him my deepest might
May the universe turn these words to truth

The Fade

Ladies and Gentlemen
The voice of a woman comes from everywhere
Is it the train announcer's voice above me?
Or the voice of God?
I'm not sure
My heart stops anyway

It's over
The voice continues
What's over?
Everything begins to fade away

I run the other way
But things start to fade faster
I bump into a partially faded door
What's happening?

Apocalypse is here
We weren't ready for it
Where do we go from here?
The fade will not answer

For

———— ∞ ————

Now that I know
Who I'm intended for
Designed for
Meant for
Used for
I can give up games and scores
Cause now that I know
Who I'm in favor for
On behalf for
Pro for
In support for
I can be ingeniously more
Ever since now that I know
Who I'm in lieu for
In place for
Representing for
I can get through any door

From Her Ass To Her Mouth

———— ⧜ ————

From her ass to her mouth
She was sweet
Like golden wheat
High yellow she was
Like Bart Simpson or something
I really miss pumping this one
She made me weak everywhere
I used to stare at her
Unaware of where her power lied

From her ass to her mouth
She was a princess of this world
She was a fucking goddess
Her hush-hushes looked just like island fruit
Like nectar on a table
Split in half after a cool rain
She smelled like bananas and pears, too
She was the intimate decree
I worshiped her like a yacht
I saw my name all over thee
She was there for me
The only one that was there for me

From her eyes to her clitoris
She was the diamond of her gender
I remember a day in September

I was asleep and I woke up in her cavity
Doing the deed before I understood I was doing it
She was fun like that
Her strokes
I could never forget
It was a gift from the sex angel of contact
Wow, I really miss her
She was a great stripper, too
Her abs were a killer
Sometimes she wanted to see my explosion
Get stuck in the crevices

From my heart to hers
She was the wife I should've married
She was so bad and so good at the same time
My honey went away
Why did you have to be the hero for young strippers?
My baby got shot in the head
Helping a fellow co-worker get away from her abusive boyfriend
The same damn story throughout history
Death is a waste of that fine ass, sweet Jesus, my lord
You don't know
You just don't know
Well, she lived life corrupted
This could have been a repercussion
She was happy though
That's all that matters
I'm thinking about her right now

The Hidden

Up and Upon
Beyond and yonder
Reminiscent of a dream
Low and Down
Around and surround
The undetermined entity

Close and near
Far and away
Above the treacherous sleep
Side by side
Eclipse and surpass
To see the hidden weep

Love and like
Hate and mean
Goodness strives to teach
Punish and blame
Run and chase
The lesson will commit a breach

Dance and jam
Listen and hear
The best words to feel
Cold or hot

Uncomfortable and painful
The hidden will reveal the real deal
The truth

The Unexpected Divine

Like one of our greatest kings
I had a dream, too
Walking across a windy beach
By myself until I proverb that I wasn't alone
Because I was with my queen
My only lily
She was oily and sexy
She was like a goddess closing in on me

It was a great beautiful day
That happens once in every life
We looked within our souls very hard
I thought we were doing Precalculus for a moment
Come what may in that very second,
I had another dream that meddled with the first one
Making me feel we were in a bubble or a crystal ball
Like I was being watched by something great

Easily enough, caring gave up on trying to understand
I took my lily's hand
Wrote her name with her hand in the sand
I looked at her as I cleaned off the grit
Pulled her close with the other hand
Gently from the waist form accompanying her hip
Giving her sweet nothings until she couldn't comprehend
She was where cloud nine hung time without end

We were going to stay here for a cool while
As I planned to be the keeper of all her smiles
Write her notes, paint her boats
Deliver her famous quotes
Express my love in musical notes
With me, she will be a float of light
I will be her protector of all plight

Frantic and fear become brothers at times
Looking in too deeply into something not so deep
Never doubt the unexpected divine
This is beautiful existence
This is not a dream
We were blessed like a sweet dream
We are happy in love
I know this just by the view
The outlook is wonderful
Anything could be full of wonder in how you look out

The Nameless, The Anonymous And The New

I love myself
I always have
I just can say it now
I lost myself once
Like in the woodland
I want lose myself again
Some days were harder than others
When I found myself dwelling deep into the past
But I appreciate this present
I will appreciate the future
I will embrace the nameless, the anonymous and the new
I don't have any bottled up regrets
Because I am where I am supposed to be

It feels so good to say I love myself
I appreciate the all of me now
I don't regret anything anymore
I can't change the past
I don't want to change the past
I will live for the soul of me
I know there's a God
I know there's a destiny
I know I am blessed
I know that anything I don't know will be known
I love this universe
I love this planet

I love this country
I love this city
I love this town
I love the air that keeps me breathing
I love this food that keeps me thinking
I love this water that keeps me cleansing
I love my mind
I love my body
I love my soul
The only love that I have been looking for
Is the love inside of me
I love the power in me

I love you
And if you love me,
I will love you more
I will pay you a lifetime of rewards
Just by loving you
So I will love you
Even at times, I don't like to show it
I will love people, places and things
I will love it all
I will love the nameless, the anonymous and the new
The universe loves me
The universe loves you, too

Yet To Come

---∞---

Very happy appreciating every nook of it
Oh, it feels so good
The yet to come
Let's not be nasty now
At least not this time
About this yet to come
Just loving the previous yet to come
Digging the current yet to come
Awaiting the next yet to come
Let's not be nasty now
At least not this time
About this yet to come
So ready for so much more
Sweet and special yet to come

Sundry And All

─────── ∞ ───────

We have been visiting Earth for a jiffy
Some of us are still acting petty
With that we don't know why look on the face
Wanting to really know why

Isn't it obvious that this is a test to fly?
Not like birds or spacecrafts
Not like liquor or preparation habits
Just the ultimate soar to success
To succeed amongst sundry and all

We still get it wrong every awaken day
We don't know how to do a 360 as of yet
Soon we will drop the idiot pills
Come on and get back in the race
We have a lot to mentally taste

We all have souls
A special sole purpose my friends
On this Earth today
To be the most alive we could be
When we were born,
We signed a sanctified agreement with one
The universe

With simple details of what we are meant to do
What makes us think our light is meaningless?
What makes us think that?

We have energy to deliver
We have energy to receive
Buzz the electricity that will never shock
We are all ready a must
We are all ready done sisters and brothers
Every thing is happening as it should
Value and exult this exclusive live

The only real job that we have is to love ourselves
Feel the wraith of the great goodness
We have so much power if we would just work it right
At times, there will be the feeling of sidelines
Deliberate adversaries to strike a different chord with us
Still remember, when we were born,
We signed a sanctified agreement with one
The universe

We will never find an agreement like this again people
This one is not a con or a contract
This agreement is a winner to the very end
Until the last second of our last day
It's the only agreement we don't have to read
We just have to know that we are here for a cause
A great cause to fulfill
Cause God loves us all the time
Cause God is cool like a bathtub in the morning

The Thunder

The thunder lives
As long as the firmament lives
It's funny how someone
Could blame another someone
About something
That has nothing to do with them
Because the someone
Can't admit to themselves
That they did something so dumb
The other someone becomes the thunder

The someone wants to be mad
And fight another someone physically
When the someone is truly messing
With themselves mentally
And to mess with the other someone
Is an attempt on their mentality
The other someone is the thunder
They can't be affected
They can't be destroyed

There will always be people
That can't stand who you are
What someone does to the other someone
Has nothing to do with them
It has to do with themselves

Children's Book

It's either envy or jealousy
Making the thunder work like labor
The thunder lives
As long as the firmament lives

The Coveted Kiss

To taste her smile,
I want

The coveted kiss,
I want

Like a rose,
She should have

She wants to be desired,
I want to give her a rose

Get her to kiss me harmoniously,
Taste her smile

To yearn a coveted moment,
See her psyche work

Spineless Hatchling

————— ∞ —————

If I wait on you, I fail with you
Sorry woman
You don't run this farm
You don't run this haunt
You ain't nothing but a wretched hatchling
Dreadfully sad to have spinelessness all damn day

Self-centered, hypocritical hatchling
Get in the pecking order concerning my penis, my dream
You don't succeed at anything
You just sabotage yourself
Wake up and smell the new coffee

Just like the spineless hatchling
Tells you one thing, does another
Why do I waste seeds on your bill?
Why can't you produce affirmative eggs?
What excuse do you have today?
Who will you accuse later?
A spineless hatchling always find something to say
Why don't you say you're a spineless hatchling?
That's what I'm waiting to hear

Sweetheart Person

Sexy, pretty, nasty
Strapping resembling a beat
Sweetheart person with a will of good nut prickle
Feeling alive with chains and whips
Mixed flora of falling slither and feather
Dangerous juicy full of fun
Succulent wily full-grown of warm heat
Bonbon sly, shy of eighteen
Voice mad and calm together
Leather gloves and lace
Convinced positions with fruition
Black masked face and wounded lips red
Nine to five working nights in the bayou

The Universe

———— ∞ ————

These dreams otherwise known as reality
Fantasy about a naked superstar in the streets of Harlem
No one around, but I feel alive with her
Looking at her nipples and liking it
I wake up like I kissed them for a long time
And felt they were sweet
I must be batty
Knowing that she's dead in her true place of existence
So many dreams of being friends
Having fun at the movies or something
I can't remember it all
I try to remember the whole story
Still don't know if I am to join her in the dead
Just don't know
Sometimes, I don't care
But I fight these dreams sometimes
Wondering why I feel so sexual for the deceased
Something to do with the universe, my universe
Wondering if it's punishing me or rewarding me
I want to tell the universe to stop
That I had enough
I'm hoping the universe will strengthen me
Empower me
Make me more knowledgeable
Make me as mentally powerful
As physically powerful is the sun

I hope the universe is rewarding me
I want to be like the universe
I want to be one whole like you

The Novel

———— ∞ ————

Yesterday, I was reading this book
The main character had your name
She met this guy on a boulevard in Virginia
Didn't I meet you on a boulevard in Virginia?
I kept reading and the book is doing,
What we did in real life
I get scared and horny
I don't know
But I wanted to call you
I resisted, we haven't spoken in a minute

We never talked about us,
But let's talk about us
Let's talk about this book for a minute
Do you know the author?
The book just came out
This book is about us somewhat
Do you know the publisher?
What's going on?
We fall in love in the book
We will fall in love in real life?

Maybe if you read this author's book,
You could better decide
Don't hide, just glide between the words
In this novel

I don't like books written about me
When I don't know the author
So talk to me after you get to page 323

I'm going back to the future
To understand the make up
I want to take up the book's lone purpose
I had this reality you wanted me
Where's your reality at, huh?
Help me figure this literary blues
Unite the clues and the rules
Stop looking at me and read that book

Oh, you know how I got that book?
Someone threw it at me as I was getting on the train
The cop tried to chase me instead of the attacker
I fell down, he fell down
Knocked over a bunch of people
I was heated mad because the injury smarts
The book appealed to me after it all
I started reading it
I have been resisting everything except today
That's why I know we have to talk
Could we rap over a few breakfasts and dinners?

The Unutterable Article

Right through the windows
Icy hell in the region
Summer hell inside this manor
Drinking to stay cool
Near the bathroom
The coolest place to chill

The mood begins to substitute
Ideas of serious gender tapping
Darn temperature creating some aggravated rudeness
The maid had to take today off
Love screams to be torn

Look somewhere else
Don't incite a reason
The thirst subversion
Panties too close to pull down easy
Walk away or become uninviting
Do something
This can't happen today

It's almost like seeing a mirage
In which the assimilated apple split is asking
To come on over and interrupt this unproductiveness
Pheromone secretions in the air all ready
The scuba diver is putting its gear on

Close the shower door real tight
It's going to get extra wet in here
The unutterable article in black and white
By neuromuscular tensions

Willpower

———— ∞ ————

If you guess your willpower,
Your power will guess

If you doubt your willpower,
Your power will doubt

If you don't have willpower,
Your power won't have none

If you have willpower,
Your power will have will

Whore World

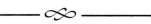

World look at yourself
It's a whore world

Everywhere is pimping people
It's a whore world

The venal is selling people
It's a whore world after all

The Challenge

———— ∞ ————

I challenge you to think differently
I challenge you to think with mental fruition
I challenge you to make dreams reality
I challenge you to breathe without air
To live in your true nature
To live within your real self
Without fear of yourself or anyone else

I challenge you to choose wisely
Between an idea or a belief
Which is better?
Which is worse?
An idea never hurts anyone
But a belief can create wars around the world
The problem with this world thus far
Is we haven't done the exchange

I challenge you to find better possibilities
Life is a book and I'm the author of mine
Are you the author of your book?
If you're not the author, who's writing you?
Your friends?
Your parents?
Your lover?
Your job?
Your neighbors?

Your past?
Your failures?
Write the pages yourself
Make the story all by yourself
Put in whatever it is you want
Or whatever it is you want to happen
Better yet, put in whatever it is you need

First things first
Do you know what kind of book are you?
I'm a children's book
Choose your book
Is this still really a challenge I'm giving you?
Or a favor?
Better that, how about a reminder?
In the greater world of this world,
You made an agreement to live life to the fullest
Finally, I challenge you to challenge others
To think differently

Plot Of You

───────── ∞ ─────────

From the start,
I've been a part of your genuine heart
You've done your best to miss all my darts
But I hit you so swift, you're kind of tart
And just like the museum,
That displays your art
It imparts you
I also impart you
I'm a part of the plot of you

The Terror Campaign

When the big remonstration was roughly speaking
All streets of Manhattan was heaving with law
Walked through the hot spot
To make way to see a friend in the hospital
With a gift box of hidden books in hold
Everywhere the law stared at it
The terror campaign had begun
Not thinking of trouble
Nevertheless trouble continued on
Anticipated so much confrontation
A very loud noise bursted open
From the remonstration and not the gift box

Bound Aries

Without Aries in the wild
I can walk further outward
I have no fear
I have no doubt anymore

I can run when I want to
I'm not running for my life
I see what's ahead
I see where I'm going
I'm finally living my life

Knowing I just bound Aries
I won't be slowed down again
I will move to the greatest heights
I will reach my prime and pivotal position
In the lead on the power board of time

I set Leo free to eat Aries
With all Aries to come
We will bound them all
Nix all the bound Aries

The Ravage

———— ∞ ————

Part of the turn on
Is thinking you are cabbage
Don't mind my savage
Just full of baggage
Sweet love luggage
Hope you are ready for the ravage

Why the ravage?
It's part of the turn on
The get on, the get off
To get you off
Nice and soft
In this paradise loft
Furnished in the delicate riches of cloth
The ravage starts now
Excuse your face
I want you near the ruby vase
Let the ravage swallow you up

It is not too early
It's never too early for sex
It's never too late
This is sexual payback baby
Getting me this crazy on Wednesday
If you get pregnant,
Let's call the baby that day

That would be decent
Stop, I'm getting the camera
I want you to watch this later
Yes, you
You can erase it after the sixth after
Yes, you know it
I'm confident
I'm a Leo

The Slavery Of Freedom

After the slaves were freed,
The freed slaves feel before they were freed
We are still looking up at wishing moons
We are still looking up at wishing suns
As much as we fight for change,
The world is the same

How many leaders have we lost?
How many leaders will we lose?
Does freedom really exist?
We are animals to most people
All these years, we escaped from cages
Just to escape from bigger cages
How long will freedom feel like slavery?

When we dream, we often get hurt
The numbers are against us
Listen to the radio
Check out CNN
Do you see what's happening?
Death for our people is like a gift
They are killing us so fast

Our heartache and tears on cable
Or else hyperlinked on cyber news
Up and down it hits the splinter of the nation

People talk of change all the time
We have to do this
We have to do that
It's like gossip sort of
Nothing is still the result

We have prayed to God
We have walked with Seraphim angels
We have spoken to our ancestral spirits
All this and evil is still visually triumphant
Is violence the answer?
That's when will real change take place

We will still pray to God
We will still walk with Seraphim angels
We will still speak to our spirits
We will still wait
Maybe not so patiently

Eating Place

My stomach was messing with me
So I excused myself from company
Ran up two flights of stairs
To drop a load in their bathroom
As I was waiting to finish
Guys were coming in and out
Calling women bitches and so forth
Then I heard a woman outside the door

She was saying to some other women
She was coming in
She had to go bad
I heard this woman come in our bathroom
I heard a man come in, too
He wanted to know what was going on
She told him that she had to go bad
As she unfastened her jeans

In the next toilet by me,
I heard the noise of her waste
And through the crack of my door
Looking into the reflection of the mirror
I saw the man
He was holding her door open
He was watching her as she did her thing
He wanted her phone number

He wanted to shake her hand, too
He wanted to show her respect for her boldness
She said she couldn't do that
She ran out
He went after her
I was finished
I went back to my company

Transit

So what is it with you today?
Why won't you let me go my way?
I swipe and swipe
You give me delay
You say please swipe again
I'm like come on?
No freaking way
I swipe too fast
I swipe too slow
Why are you getting so sexual?
Are you transit hot?
I swipe again
You let me in
I must have swiped just right
Like a climax
The turnstile got off on my metrocard
I feel so used
I can't look at myself right now
I hate feeling used

The Messenger

———— ∞ ————

Have another helping of poetry
As I kick the real over this jazz tune
Spill out the truth over harmonic metaphors
Reverse fiction into fact
Spiritually artifact my life to your tribute
Be a rascal to a hurricane
In this little spot
Make you annoyed with my verbal plot
Check it
I was reborn to be the messenger for you
You hear me now
I don't want to hear you
You have a plane to catch after this set
I bet you regret not coming with me to tibet
Don't be upset
I wouldn't have enjoyed myself if you were there
You are just a pain in my hair
All you do is stress the unstressed
I think you want to be depressed
No one will buy your counterfeited troubles
So you better sell them to the plants on the double
They will listen
I won't glisten

All The Mirrors

Just looking at yourself
Everywhere you go
You see you in everything
You don't see people walking
You don't see people talking
You still seeing you in them
You can't keep any friends like that
You can't fall in love like that

The world is cold with ones like you
Living in the hate of the past
Is how you became hardhearted yesteryear
They aren't thinking about you
They aren't dreaming about you
Like you feel they are still
How did you get messed up like this?
Why do you see you in anything alive?

Just staying to yourself
In the dark apartment
In the remains of your regret
Lonely in the skin dust of wind
Human traces of you floating like sin
The filth in your mind like dangerous weather
Growing old with no echoes of sound
Reflections of despair is your fate

Children's Book

You can't admit that you desire to redirect
If you have newspapers,
You can cover yourself up
All the mirrors aren't helping you

,

You Will Be Life

To understand life
Is to stand under life
Because life understands you
You must live under life
Or be the word alive
Or the definition of alive
Which is having life

Having life is to enjoy life
To enjoy life is to be a life
To be a life is to be what you truly are
What you were born to do
Destiny will not begin
Until you stand under life
Be about life

To understand life
Is to stand under life
Because life understands you
Once you understand that
You must understand
To stop misunderstanding to understand
When you don't ever have to understand life
You will be life

The Queendom

My little friendly girl
Bring to a halt the asking
About the bad things
Go all-out for the good things
Broken leg, sore body, cuts and rashes
You won't be this way too long
You are arising to your full potential
You are going to achieve the gifts of dreams
You are getting to that place called the ultimate person
Are you prepared to rule over the queendom?
The queendom of you?
Don't you see your empire?
The castle?
The clothes?
The respect?
The worship?
The crown?
You will not need any help with your crown

Part Of Love

———— ∞ ————

In it all day
Still not tired
Glazed donut kiss and makeup
Yogurt sampler
Just part of love
Tomorrow, this will be in the diary
Including the dairy attempt and peanut butter
Including the salad preparation and the dressing
The belly thing, too
Just part of love
Inside the heaven of elemental sin
Just part of love, okay?

Six Days

If you found out that you were going to die
In six days,
What would you do?
Would you have a pity party?
Would you celebrate?
Could you be happy?
Death is an angel
That travels here everyday
To pick up one of us
Would you cry a bit?
Don't have time for that
Only five days left
Would you cry again?
Just wasting time
Did you forget?
You will be dead in three days
Don't worry about the time left
Celebrate what you have still
Be happy
You're not really dying
You're just moving on
To the better
Make a toast to the better
Death is like releasing energy
Like electricity, in and out of a computer
Isn't electricity a gift?

Followed by the angel of death is a gift
If you don't agree,
Just make the best of life

The Desert

Summon yourself
To be as one
In a place for one
The desert
Take these many demons
That curse your future
That haunts your soul
That objects your past
Take these many demons
Set them free within the desert
Let them fly away
Cleanse the very deepest mind
Then, await a transformation
Turn the demons into angels
Let these new symbols of yourself
Fly back to you and nurture the lost
Which now has found the new awareness
These angels will be your guide through life
You will be very well now on and after

Never Underestimate The Power

Our yourselves
It will empower
It will tower
Fresher than nutmeg flower
The virtual power
It will shower
In the zero hour
The radiant power
Exclusive of cower
It will not sour
It's definitely not dour
It's the power
Never underestimate the power of
Our yourselves

Dream Of An Impeccable Earth

———— ∞ ————

Distinguished consciousness awoken me this morning
First whiff I smelled was self-government
The second whiff I smelled was summertime
First sound I heard was a sweet union
A union of parades across the lands and oceans
A celebration of smiles like I could never imagine
My dream came true
At last, an impeccable Earth

Love won last night
Evil didn't have a chance
A spiritual revolution was on the rise for awhile
The color of all people joined together
And marshaled The Devil away
A force field was launched distributing world peace
My true purpose is the reward of being
At last, the impeccable reality

Down with hunger anywhere
Down with violence
Down with imbalanced wealth
Down with shy sty world leaders
Down with absolute sin
We rule ourselves
The real world will begin
We're all the same

We're all one
Under the denominator of love
Over the numerator of love
That's one
Life is sweeter for all of us forever
Here on this impeccable Earth
Thank you God
Thank you Jesus
Thank you love

About the Author

Gene Geter lives in New York City and this is his fourth poetry book. For more information about Gene, visit GENEGETER.COM online.

0-595-22705-8

Printed in the United States
4831